Revision: A structur

Catherine Owen and

GCSE Geography Teachers' Toolkit
Series editor: Jane Ferretti

Editor's introduction

The aims and learning outcomes of the GCSE specifications for geography should 'provide the opportunity for students to understand more about the world, the challenges it faces and their place within it. The GCSE course will deepen understanding of geographical processes, illuminate the impact of change and of complex people-environment interactions, highlight the dynamic inter-relationships and links between places and environments at different scales, and develop students' competence in using a wide range of geographical investigative skills and approaches. Geography enables young people to become globally and environmentally informed and thoughtful, enquiring citizens' (DfE, 2014).

The subject content is more prescriptive than in the past and includes physical, human and environmental processes, map skills, locational knowledge and fieldwork and an emphasis on the geography of the UK. This provides an opportunity to update and reinvigorate the geography taught at key stage 4.

The *GCSE Geography Teachers' Toolkit* series is the work of an experienced and respected team of authors, each responding creatively and imaginatively, and in a range of teaching styles, to the potential of the GCSE specifications. It is a rich source of teacher-to-teacher advice – a conversation between professionals about how to make best use of the opportunities that arise when drawing up new schemes of work.

Each title in the series provides one full unit of work: a bank of ten lesson ideas and accompanying downloadable resources. Each lesson includes key questions to engage learners and provides opportunities for them to practise the skills required to tackle GCSE examinations. The lessons are designed to be thought-provoking and we hope you use them either as set out or modified to suit the classes you teach. We also hope you will be encouraged to use the suggested teaching strategies elsewhere in the curriculum.

The supporting resources include PowerPoints, activity sheets and weblinks, all of which can be used as suggested or modified to suit your needs and the needs of your students. The resources can be downloaded from a password-protected area on the Geographical Association's website. Details of how to access these resources are given inside the front cover.

New titles, including this one, have been added to the *GCSE Geography Teachers' Toolkit* series to supplement it in light of the changes made to the specifications. Each will help teachers develop effective schemes of work appropriate to their chosen specification, focusing particularly on how GCSE geography can be taught so that students are enthused, engaged and motivated by it – thinking and acting as geographers.

Jane Ferretti, January 2016

Contents

Introduction

Changes to GCSE geography have brought both challenges and opportunities for teachers and students. The focus on knowledge means that there is a great deal for students to learn for their exams, but this constructs strong foundations on which they can build as geographers. All GCSE specifications now need to cover a core of content specified by the Department for Education (see DfE, 2014), bringing a greater consistency to GCSE courses. Changes to assessment mean that students need to be prepared to answer questions on their fieldwork experiences rather than writing controlled assessments or coursework related to these experiences.

The aim of this Toolkit is to support geography teachers in preparing their students for the GCSE geography exams. The Toolkit is organised around the themes of the DfE core content required in all the GCSE specifications and page 6 shows how this maps to the content of each GCSE specification. There are ten topics in this Toolkit - seven content topics, plus geographical skills, fieldwork and case studies.

Three lessons are provided for each topic. These are described in spreads in this book (one spread covers three lessons) and a PowerPoint presentation is provided for each topic as part of the accompanying online resources. Key resources for lessons can be printed from the slides in the PowerPoint presentation or the activity sheets, also in the online resources. The three lessons for most of the topics follow the same structure:

Introductory lesson

1. Stimulus activity to get students thinking back to the topic.
2. Students rate the relevant content in the specification they are following as either red, amber or green (RAG-ing) to show their confidence with the topic.
3. A range of revision activities then follows to review the core content of the topic.
4. Questioning should be used to check and deepen knowledge and understanding and tackle misconceptions. You may wish to plan your questions before the lesson, including who you will address them to, considering different groups in your class. You can also use questions to relate the activities more specifically to the requirements of your specification and the case studies and examples you have studied.
5. The consolidation activity will involve a knowledge recap, providing low-threat, regular testing.

Second lesson - focus on answering extended questions

1. Stimulus activity to recap a piece of key knowledge from the topic.
2. Students look back at their RAG-ing from the previous lesson, identifying areas of weakness.
3. Four possible example GCSE questions are suggested for the topic - students should choose one they are not confident about and plan an answer using their notes, textbook and/or revision guide, then answer the question.
4. Advice is provided about how to tackle the exam question, how to structure the answer using PEE (make a clear **p**oint; **e**xplain the point; give an **e**xample) and the meaning of command words.
5. You will need to let students know how many marks the question would be worth as this varies between specifications; e.g. for AQA extended questions are worth 6 or 9 marks.
6. Sentence starters for one of the questions are provided - these can be used to support students who are struggling with answering the questions, or with those who need help with structuring or developing their answers.
7. A simplified, generic mark scheme is provided so that students can self or peer assess their answers and make improvements if necessary.
8. The consolidation activity refers students back to their RAG-ing and asks them to plan their home learning to improve areas needing development. This puts the responsibility in their hands - this is *their* GCSE.

Third lesson - summarising the topic and using SAM

1 Stimulus activity to recap a piece of key knowledge from the topic.
2 Use a Sample Assessment Material (SAM) from your awarding organisation to check your students' knowledge and understanding.
3 An additional extended question is included for you to use if you have already used all the SAMs from your awarding organisation.
4 Students should then complete a revision poster/ knowledge organiser for the topic. This is likely to be started in the lesson and completed at home.
5 A generic outline for a revision poster/knowledge organiser is included in the accompanying PowerPoint, but this will need to be adapted to suit your specification.
6 The consolidation activity again asks students what they need to do to revise this topic at home and to prepare for their exams.
7 Feedback following use of the SAM may be through marking of individual scripts, but it is a good idea to use a whole class feedback grid to note general strengths and areas for development so these can be tackled with the whole class. Time should be provided for making improvements to answers.

You may not have the time to use all 30 lessons provided in this Toolkit, but can adapt the lessons and resources to suit the needs of your classes. If you are short of time you could prioritise the use of the first lesson from each set of three, then use the choice of six-mark questions for students to answer as a homework activity. The case studies lessons (pages 32-33) could be missed out as other case studies will have already been tackled through topics. If more time is available in lessons, students could spend it on activities such as the revision posters/knowledge organisers, or ideas from the 'Further teaching ideas' section on pages 34-35 could be integrated into the revision programme. You will also need to check the requirements of your specification to ensure any additional activities are planned into your revision programme, such as work on pre-release materials.

A range of additional lesson and homework activities are also included with this Toolkit; these are intended to be useful for teachers who would like to adjust some of the lessons and also to provide students with specific homework tasks. However, it is implicit throughout this Toolkit that the work in the lesson must be complemented by students' revision and work at home, without which many of the lessons will not be as effective as they could be.

Teachers are professionals and are responsible for providing a revision programme putting their students in the best position to succeed in the GCSE examinations. The aim of this Toolkit is to support teachers, providing resources that can be adapted and developed to suit the needs of their individual contexts and classes. These resources may be delivered as a whole revision scheme of learning, dipped into to complement a school's own revision scheme of learning or used throughout the GCSE course to support students in preparing for end-of-topic tests and pre-public exams.

GCSE specification coverage

This Toolkit is suitable for use across all specifications. The exam-style practice questions are not taken from the Sample Assessment Material (SAM) provided by each awarding organisation but have been written for this resource. It is expected that you will refer to the SAMs and mark schemes for your own specification.

1: Locational knowledge and map skills

AQA	Geographical applications
OCR A	Geographical skills
OCR B	Geographical skills
Edexcel A	Component 3
Edexcel B	3: Making a geographical decision
Eduqas A	Component 3
Eduqas B	2: Problem-solving geography

2: Fieldwork and use of data

AQA	Geographical applications
OCR A	Geographical skills
OCR B	Our natural world and People and Skills
Edexcel A	Component 3
Edexcel B	2: Geographical investigations
Eduqas A	Component 3
Eduqas B	Component 3

3: Geomorphic processes and landscape

AQA	Living with the physical environment; Physical landscapes in the UK
OCR A	Living in the UK today; Landscapes of the UK
OCR B	Our natural world; Distinctive landscapes
Edexcel A	1: The changing landscapes of the UK
Edexcel B	2: The UK's evolving physical landscape
Eduqas A	1: Landscapes and physical processes; 2: Coastal hazards and their management
Eduqas B	1: Changing environments

4: Changing weather and climate

AQA	Living with the physical environment; The challenge of natural hazards
OCR A	Living in the UK today; UK environmental challenges; The world around us; Environmental threats to our planet
OCR B	Our natural world; Global hazards and Changing climate
Edexcel A	1: Weather hazards and climate change
Edexcel B	1: Hazardous Earth
Eduqas A	2: Weather, climate and ecosystems
Eduqas B	1: Changing environments

5: Global ecosystems and biodiversity

AQA	Living with the physical environment; The living world
OCR A	The world around us; Ecosystems of the planet
OCR B	Our natural world; Sustaining ecosystems
Edexcel A	1: Ecosystems, biodiversity and management
Edexcel B	3: People and the biosphere and Forests under threat
Eduqas A	2: Weather, climate and ecosystems
Eduqas B	1: Environmental challenges

6: Resources and their management

AQA	Challenges in the human environment; The challenge of resource management
OCR A	Living in the UK today; UK environmental challenges
OCR B	People and society; Resource resilience
Edexcel A	2: Resource management
Edexcel B	3: Consuming energy resources
Eduqas A	2: Development and resource issues
Eduqas B	1: Environmental challenges

7: Cities and urban society

AQA	Challenges in the human environment; Urban issues and challenges
OCR A	Living in the UK today; People of the UK and The world around us; People of the planet
OCR B	People and society; Urban futures
Edexcel A	2: Changing cities
Edexcel B	1: Challenges of an urbanising world and 2: The UK's evolving human landscape
Eduqas A	1: Rural-urban links
Eduqas B	1: Changing places: changing economies

8: Global economic and development issues

AQA	Challenges in the human environment; The changing economic world
OCR A	The world around us; People of the planet
OCR B	People and society; Urban futures
Edexcel A	2: Global development
Edexcel B	1: Development dynamics and 2: The UK's evolving human landscape
Eduqas A	2: Development and resource issues
Eduqas B	1: Changing places: changing economies

9: Tectonic hazards

AQA	Living with the physical environment; The challenge of natural hazards
OCR B	Our natural world; Global hazards
Eduqas A	Tectonic landscapes and hazards

10: Case studies

AQA, OCR A, OCR B, Edexcel A, Edexcel B, Eduqas A, Eduqas B	All specifications

Medium term plan

Lesson/key questions	Learning objectives	Teaching and learning activities	Resources	DfE GCSE subject content
Locational knowledge and map skills How are places linked? How can maps show us important geographical information?	To identify gaps in locational knowledge and map skills To practise map skills To assess understanding of locational knowledge and map skills.	**Lesson 1** Students add continents and key places to a world map. They RAG their understanding of this topic and then make links between different places. There is a team challenge using case study cards. Students reflect on the use of GIS to obtain, illustrate, analyse and evaluate geographical information. **Lesson 2** Students identify the location of case studies. They answer a series of questions using an OS map extract. Students reassess their RAG-ing from Lesson 1 to prepare for Lesson 3. **Lesson 3** Students complete a true or false quiz. They complete an exam question to assess this element of the course. Students create a revision poster for this topic then reflect on their individual areas of strength and weakness.	Activity sheets 1, 2, 3 and 4 PowerPoint 1: Locational knowledge and map skills	1 Locational knowledge: 8. 2 Maps, fieldwork and geographical skills: 10. maps Appendix: Cartographic skills
Fieldwork and use of data What geographical concepts were explored in fieldwork? What research methods were used? What data was collected?	To identify gaps in knowledge of fieldwork techniques To practise selected fieldwork techniques To revise aspects of students' own fieldwork To assess understanding of fieldwork techniques	**Lesson 1** Students draw a field sketch from memory. They RAG their understanding of this topic, and prepare for a fieldwork interview. Students develop ideas about data and complete a short statistics quiz. Students reflect on the question: 'How could you statistically confirm whether house prices decrease with distance from the CBD in an urban area?' **Lesson 2** Students match graph types to graph names. They complete a sequence of tasks based on fieldwork exam questions. Students reassess their RAG-ing from Lesson 1 to prepare for Lesson 3. **Lesson 3** The class completes a short quiz on fieldwork. Students complete an exam question to assess this element of the course. They design a revision poster for this topic then reflect on their individual areas of strength and weakness.	Activity sheets 5, 6 and 7 PowerPoint 2: Fieldwork and use of data	2 Maps, fieldwork and geographical skills: 11. Fieldwork 12. Use of data 13. Formulating enquiry and argument Appendix: Graphical skills Numerical skills Statistical skills

Lesson/key questions	Learning objectives	Teaching and learning activities	Resources	DfE GCSE subject content
Geomorphic processes and landscape Where are areas of highland and lowland located in the UK? How do weathering, erosion, transportation and deposition shape two distinct landscapes in the UK? How do these processes lead to the formation of distinctive landforms? How and why are UK landscapes managed?	To identify gaps in knowledge of geomorphic processes and landscape To reinforce key concepts and examples To practise extended answers for this topic To assess understanding of geomorphic processes and landscape	**Lesson 1** Students draw a UK landscape map from memory. They RAG their understanding of this topic, then review erosion, transportation and deposition processes. They think of actions to match the processes, then complete diagrams and work with photos to consolidate knowledge about landform formation and landscape management. Students complete a quick quiz on the UK physical landscape. **Lesson 2** Students review the actions they came up with in Lesson 1. They choose and answer one of four exam questions, then peer assess using a simplified mark scheme. Students reassess their RAG-ing from Lesson 1 to prepare for Lesson 3. **Lesson 3** Students think of a question about one of the UK landscapes studied, which is asked of another student. Students design a revision poster for this topic, and complete an exam question to assess this element of the course. Students reflect on their individual areas of strength and weakness.	Activity sheets 8 and 9 PowerPoint 3: Geomorphic processes and landscape	3 Place: processes and relationships: 14. Geography of the UK 4 Physical geography: processes and change: 15. Geomorphic processes and landscape
Changing weather and climate What are the causes and consequences of and responses to extreme weather conditions and hazards? How can real world examples of weather hazards be described and explained? How does the global circulation system influence weather and climate? How is climate change caused by both human and physical processes?	To identify gaps in knowledge of changing weather and climate To reinforce key concepts and examples To practise extended answers for this topic To assess understanding of changing weather and climate	**Lesson 1** Students guess at a weather hazard as it is gradually revealed. They RAG their understanding of this topic before answering questions on the global circulation system. They retell a storm hazard case study as a story, link images to climate change and describe a graph linked to climate change. Students complete a quick true or false quiz on changing weather and climate. **Lesson 2** Students draw the global circulation system on balloons, paper plates or paper. They choose and answer one of four exam questions, then peer assess using a simplified mark scheme. Students reassess their RAG-ing from Lesson 1 to prepare for Lesson 3. **Lesson 3** As a class, students complete an explanation of a hazard one word at a time. Students complete an exam question to assess this element of the course, then design a revision poster for this topic. Students reflect on their individual areas of strength and weakness.	Activity sheets 10, 11 and 12 PowerPoint 4: Changing weather and climate	4 Physical geography: processes and change: 16. Changing weather and climate

Lesson/key questions	Learning objectives	Teaching and learning activities	Resources	DfE GCSE subject content
Global ecosystems and biodiversity What are the characteristics of large-scale natural global ecosystems and how are they distributed? How are climate, soil, water, plants, animals and humans interdependent in two ecosystems? How are ecosystems used unsustainably and sustainably?	To identify gaps in knowledge of global ecosystems and biodiversity To reinforce key concepts and examples To practise extended answers for this topic To assess understanding of global ecosystems and biodiversity	**Lesson 1** Students describe ecosystem characteristics from photos. They RAG their understanding of this topic, then produce a concept mapping diagram for each ecosystem studied, including specific details. They complete a table identifying sustainable and unsustainable uses. Students undertake the food web challenge using a ball of string. **Lesson 2** Students decide which ecosystem they would prefer for different activities, and explain why. They choose and answer one of four exam questions, then peer assess using a simplified mark scheme. Students reassess their RAG-ing from Lesson 1 to prepare for Lesson 3. **Lesson 3** As a class, watch a clip of each of their ecosystems and note 5Ws. Students complete an exam question to assess this element of the course, then design a revision poster for this topic. Students reflect on their individual areas of strength and weakness.	Activity sheets 13 and 14 PowerPoint 5: Global ecosystems and biodiversity	5 People and environment: processes and interactions: 17. Global ecosystems and biodiversity
Resources and their management What are natural resources? How can resource exploitation have an impact on people and the environment? How has supply and demand for natural resources changed?	To identify gaps in knowledge of resources and their management To reinforce key concepts and examples To practise extended answers for this topic To assess understanding of resources and their management	**Lesson 1** Students develop a concept map based on their resource use and compare with a LIC example. They RAG their understanding then discuss a Gapminder resource and select either food, water or energy for specific revision activities. Students consider issues of resource exploitation. **Lesson 2** Students consider a resource-based decision. They choose and answer one of four exam questions, then peer assess using a simplified mark scheme. Students reassess their RAG-ing from Lesson 1 to prepare for Lesson 3. **Lesson 3** Students complete a simple mix and match activity. They complete an exam question to assess this element of the course, then design a revision poster for this topic. Students reflect on their individual areas of strength and weakness.	Activity sheets 15, 16 and 17 PowerPoint 6: Resources and their management	5 People and environment: processes and interactions: 18. Resources and their management

Lesson/key questions	Learning objectives	Teaching and learning activities	Resources	DfE GCSE subject content
Cities and urban society What are the causes and effects of rapid urbanisation and contrasting urban trends in different parts of the world? What is life like in two cities in two contrasting countries? What are the contemporary challenges arising from and influencing urban change in each city?	To identify gaps in knowledge of cities and urban society To reinforce key concepts and examples To practise extended answers for this topic To assess understanding of cities and urban society	**Lesson 1** Students consider factors causing urbanisation, with image prompts. They RAG their understanding of this topic, then summarise their two case studies. They produce concept maps showing the factors that influence change in their cities and compare migration stories. The class plays keyword bingo. **Lesson 2** Students suggest the odd-one-out from sets of key words. They choose and answer one of four exam questions, then peer assess using a simplified mark scheme. Students reassess their RAG-ing from Lesson 1 to prepare for Lesson 3. **Lesson 3** Students consider contexts for their two cities. Students complete an exam question to assess this element of the course, then design a revision poster for this topic. Students reflect on their individual areas of strength and weakness.	Activity sheets 18, 19 and 20 PowerPoint 7: Cities and urban society	6 Human geography: processes and change: 19. Cities and urban society
Global economic and development issues What do we mean by the term development? How uneven is the pattern of development and how has it changed over time? What are the impacts and solutions to uneven patterns of development?	To identify gaps in knowledge of global economic and development issues To reinforce key concepts and examples To practise extended answers for this topic To assess understanding of global economic and development issues	**Lesson 1** Students match images to key terms. They RAG their understanding, then identify and categorise key development indicators. They consider the causes of uneven development, and complete a sketchnote about their case study country's context. Students devise a simple development model with inputs and outputs, and discuss its limitations. **Lesson 2** Students complete a quiz about their case study country. They choose and answer one of four exam questions, then peer assess using a simplified mark scheme. Students reassess their RAG-ing from Lesson 1 to prepare for Lesson 3. **Lesson 3** Students consider development indicators for different countries, and their limitations. Students complete an exam question to assess this element of the course, then design a revision poster for this topic. Students reflect on their individual areas of strength and weakness.	Activity sheets 21 and 22 PowerPoint 8: Global economic and development issues	6 Human geography: processes and change: 20. Global economic development issues

Lesson/key questions	Learning objectives	Teaching and learning activities	Resources	DfE GCSE subject content
Tectonic hazards How do physical processes cause earthquakes and volcanic eruptions? What are the effects of, and responses to, a tectonic hazard and how they can vary between areas of contrasting levels of wealth? How can management reduce the effects of a tectonic hazard?	To identify gaps in knowledge of tectonic hazards To reinforce key concepts and examples To practise extended answers for this topic To assess understanding of tectonic hazards	**Lesson 1** Students use classroom equipment to model what happens at plate margins. They RAG their understanding, then describe and explain volcano and earthquake distribution. They complete a fact file for their tectonic hazard case study. Students consider whether they would prefer to experience a tectonic hazard in a lower or higher income country. **Lesson 2** Model slab pull using a chain. Students choose and answer one of four exam questions, then peer assess using a simplified mark scheme. Students reassess their RAG-ing from Lesson 1 to prepare for Lesson 3. **Lesson 3** Students consider potential costs and benefits of living in a tectonically-active region. Students complete an exam question to assess this element of the course, then design a revision poster for this topic. Students reflect on their individual areas of strength and weakness.	Activity sheets 23 and 24 PowerPoint 9: Tectonic hazards	This topic is not included in the GCSE core content, but is included in most GCSE geography specifications. Check your specification to see its requirements for this topic.
Case studies What are the key case studies we have studied? How do case studies link to the broader issues we have studied? What are the key physical and human features of our case studies?	To identify gaps in knowledge of case studies To reinforce key concepts and examples To practise extended answers for this topic To assess understanding of case studies	**Lesson 1** Students list their case studies and consider their importance. They RAG their understanding, then work in groups to produce a revision resource for one case study. The resources are shared. Students evaluate the revision resources. **Lesson 2** Students improve an exemplar answer. They choose and answer one of four exam questions, then peer assess using a simplified mark scheme. Students reassess their RAG-ing from Lesson 1 to prepare for Lesson 3. **Lesson 3** Students discuss when it is a good idea to refer to a case study in an exam question. Students complete an exam question to assess this element of the course, then design a revision poster for their case studies. Students reflect on their individual areas of strength and weakness.	Activity sheets 25, 26 and 27 PowerPoint 10: Case studies	Two different and distinctive landscapes in the UK Two selected ecosystems Detailed study of either food, water or energy as a resource One city in a LIC or NEE and one city in a HIC Country study of a LIC or NEE Case studies and exemplars must relate to at least two countries other than the UK

Quick guide to lesson resources

You can access all these resources and more, plus all the weblinks, on the GA website. To download your resources, log on to *www.geography.org.uk/gcsetoolkit*, then click on the button for this book. You will be asked for your password. The unique password for this book is CS18R2.

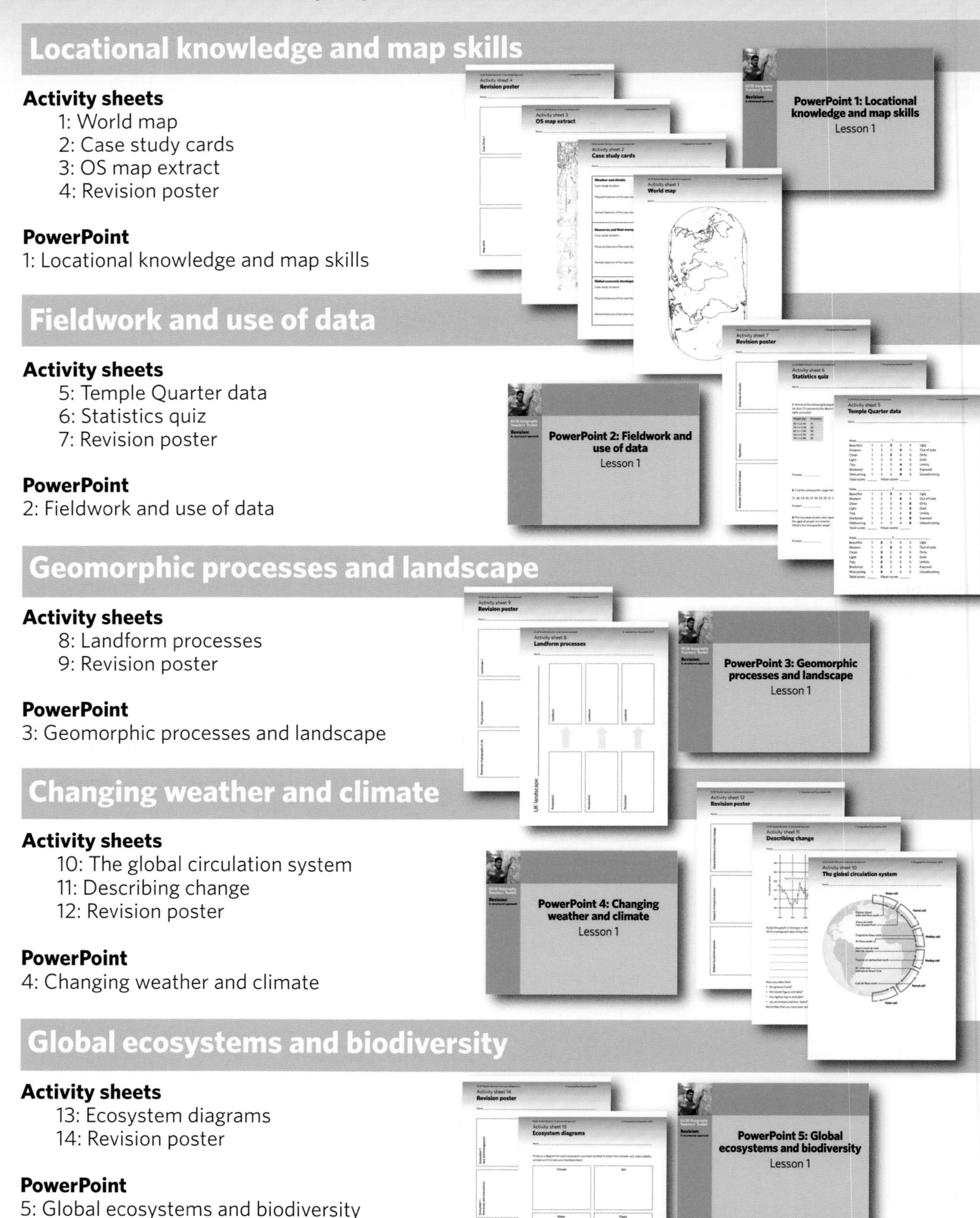

Locational knowledge and map skills

Activity sheets

1: World map
2: Case study cards
3: OS map extract
4: Revision poster

PowerPoint

1: Locational knowledge and map skills

Fieldwork and use of data

Activity sheets

5: Temple Quarter data
6: Statistics quiz
7: Revision poster

PowerPoint

2: Fieldwork and use of data

Geomorphic processes and landscape

Activity sheets

8: Landform processes
9: Revision poster

PowerPoint

3: Geomorphic processes and landscape

Changing weather and climate

Activity sheets

10: The global circulation system
11: Describing change
12: Revision poster

PowerPoint

4: Changing weather and climate

Global ecosystems and biodiversity

Activity sheets

13: Ecosystem diagrams
14: Revision poster

PowerPoint

5: Global ecosystems and biodiversity

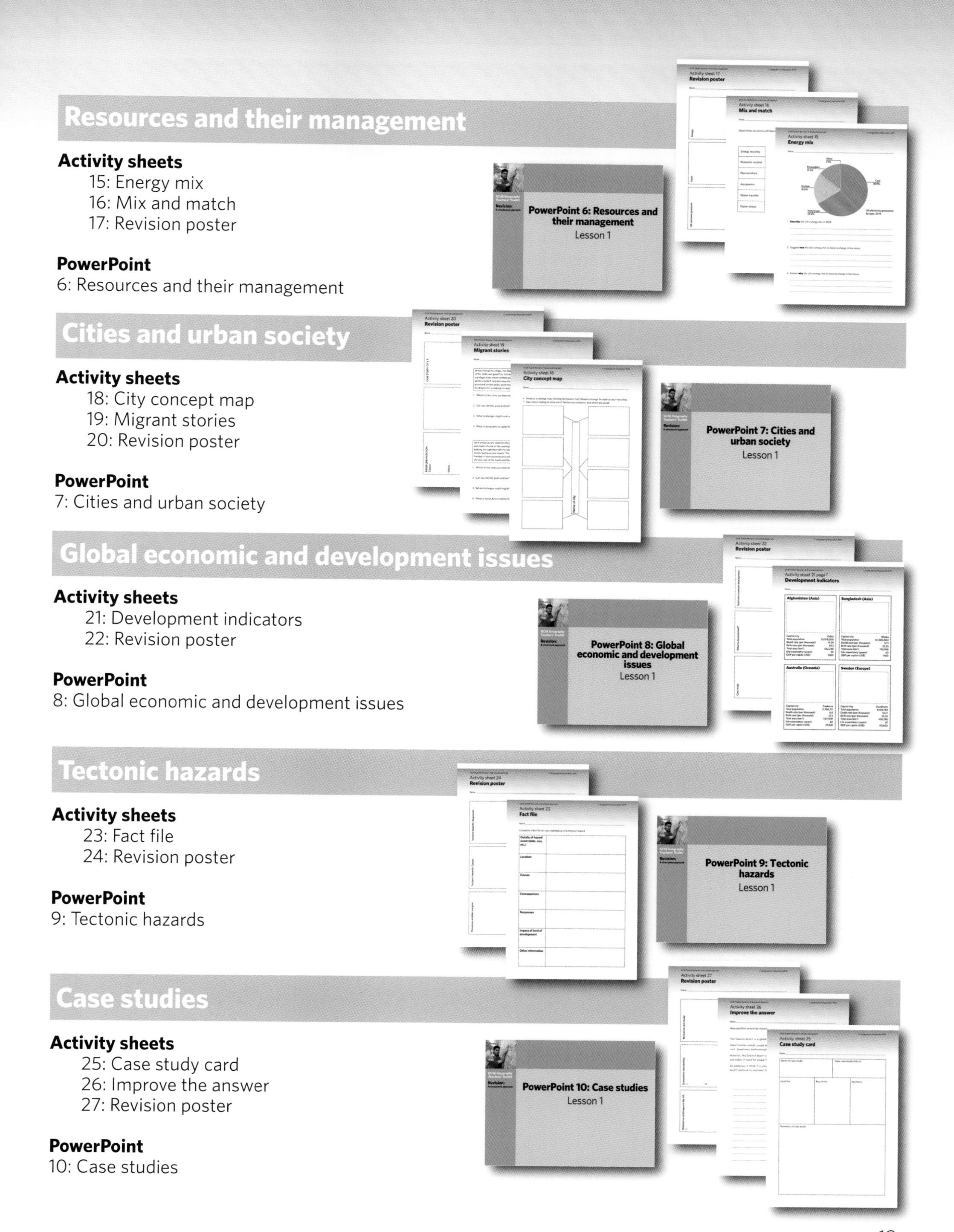

Resources and their management

Activity sheets

- 15: Energy mix
- 16: Mix and match
- 17: Revision poster

PowerPoint

6: Resources and their management

Cities and urban society

Activity sheets

- 18: City concept map
- 19: Migrant stories
- 20: Revision poster

PowerPoint

7: Cities and urban society

Global economic and development issues

Activity sheets

- 21: Development indicators
- 22: Revision poster

PowerPoint

8: Global economic and development issues

Tectonic hazards

Activity sheets

- 23: Fact file
- 24: Revision poster

PowerPoint

9: Tectonic hazards

Case studies

Activity sheets

- 25: Case study card
- 26: Improve the answer
- 27: Revision poster

PowerPoint

10: Case studies

Locational knowledge and map skills

Key questions

- How are places linked?
- How can maps show us important geographical information?

Learning objectives

- To identify gaps in locational knowledge and map skills
- To practise map skills
- To assess understanding of locational knowledge and map skills

Resources

- Activity sheets
  - 1: World map
  - 2: Case study cards
  - 3: OS map extract
  - 4: Revision poster
- PowerPoint
  - 1: Locational knowledge and map skills

Lesson 1

Stimulus

As a class, look at the world map on **PowerPoint 1**, slide 2 (also available as **Activity sheet 1**). Students should be engaged in a discussion and class activity to add continents and key places. Students should be encouraged to think about countries and the physical/environmental/ human features used from the case studies they have studied. Students will be tested on these in Lesson 3.

Development

Students carry out a RAG-ing activity to identify areas of strength and areas for development by colour coding statements from the relevant specification, which you will need to provide (instructions on **PowerPoint 1**, slide 3). Students will refer back to this document several times, so it needs to be kept in a safe place.

Look at the map from the stimulus activity. Students should suggest ways that the places shown are linked and related to other places locally, regionally, nationally and globally (**PowerPoint 1**, slide 4). This will encourage them to discuss the interdependence of places. Students should then write a sentence for each location shown on the map to set it in context.

Next, students should complete the team challenge using case study cards (see **PowerPoint 1**, slides 5-6, and **Activity sheet 2**) and resources in the classroom, such as OS maps, atlases and textbooks.

Consolidation

Students should reflect on using GIS to obtain, illustrate, analyse and evaluate geographical information. The teacher should explore this using the following whole class questioning technique: pose the question, pause for students to consider, pounce on a student to answer the question and then bounce to another student to develop the answer (**PowerPoint 1**, slide 7 sets this out so you can introduce your students to the process or remind them of how it works).

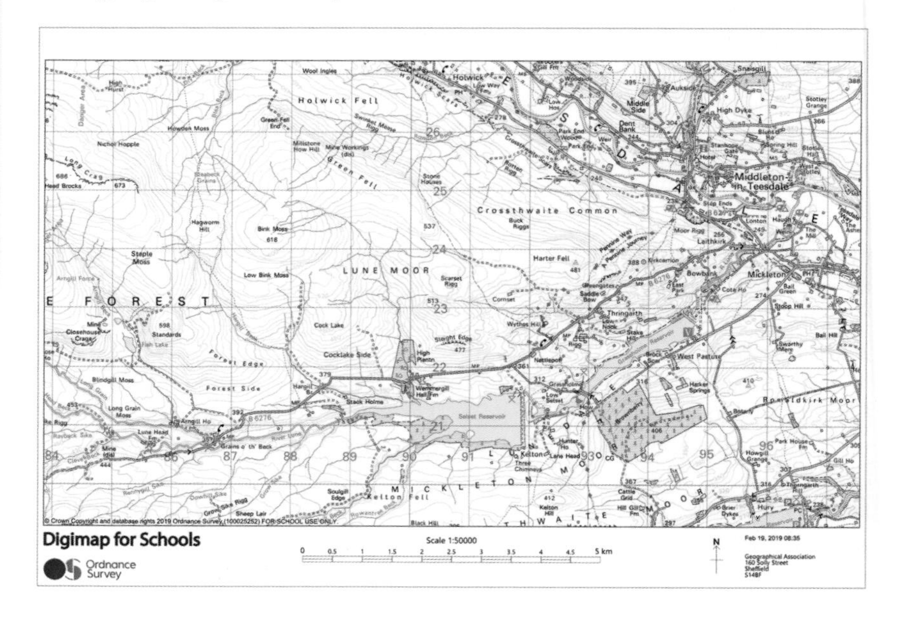

Lesson 2

Stimulus

Look at **PowerPoint 1**, slide 9 as a class. Ask students to come up to identify the location of the case studies that meet the criteria on the PowerPoint.

Development

Students answer the following questions (also on **PowerPoint 1**, slide 10) using the map extract provided on **Activity sheet 3** (also **PowerPoint 1**, slide 11).

1. What is the land use at grid reference 9321? (Answer: woodland/transport/leisure/water storage.)
2. What is the six-figure grid reference for Lune Head Farm? (Answer: 859208.)
3. Describe the main human features of the area shown in the OS map extract. (Answer: town of Middleton-in-Teesdale in the north east, reservoirs to the south of Lune Moor.)
4. What direction would you be travelling in between Wythes Hill (9222) and Harker Springs (9421)? (Answer: south east.)
5. What is the relief of the land like at 8522? (Answer: a steep incline from Fish Lake.)

Students peer assess their answers (**PowerPoint 1**, slide 12) and use this to identify any gaps in their knowledge and understanding. They then use their notes and useful books and websites to master these skills.

Consolidation

Students review their RAG rating from Lesson 1 using **PowerPoint 1**, slide 14. What do they need to do to prepare for an assessment next lesson?

Lesson 3

Stimulus

Use the true or false quiz (**PowerPoint 1**, slide 16) as a piece of formative assessment. Depending on the students' responses, it may be worth revisiting previous tasks or providing students with extra revision time. The correct answers are given on slide 17.

Development

Use a skills question from your awarding organisation SAM or a legacy exam paper to assess this element of the course. Also give students a blank world map (**Activity sheet 1**) and ask them again to add the case studies and examples from the map created in lesson 1. Students should then peer assess this task against the maps created in Lesson 1.

The students can then create a revision poster for this topic (see **PowerPoint 1**, slides 19–20 and **Activity sheet 4**).

Consolidation

Ask students to think about their own individual areas of strength and weakness (show slide 21). What else do they need to do to prepare for this element of the exam?

> **Teaching tips**
>
> - Mapping case studies is a useful way of both organising information when revising and providing locational context.
> - This scheme of learning uses both summative and formative assessment to inform students and their teacher about progress and understanding.
> - Metacognitive tasks that inform students about what they need to know are some of the most impactful when closing the gap for PP students.

Fieldwork and use of data

Key questions
- What geographical concepts were explored in fieldwork?
- What research methods were used?
- What data was collected?

Learning objectives
- To identify gaps in knowledge of fieldwork techniques
- To practise selected fieldwork techniques
- To revise aspects of students' own fieldwork
- To assess understanding of fieldwork techniques

Resources
- Activity sheets
  - 5: Temple Quarter data
  - 6: Statistics quiz
  - 7: Revision poster
- PowerPoint
  - 2: Fieldwork and use of data

Lesson 1

Stimulus
Show **PowerPoint 2**, slide 2. In which contrasting environments did students carry out their fieldwork? From memory, students draw sketches to show the key features of the two environments. You may need to remind students of the requirements of a field sketch. Which directions were they facing? What key processes were they observing? What makes these environments contrasting?

Development
Students carry out a RAG-ing activity to identify areas of strength and areas for development by colour coding statements from the relevant specification, which you will need to provide (instructions on **PowerPoint 2**, slide 3). Students will refer back to this document several times, so it needs to be kept in a safe place.

In groups, students prepare for a two-minute 'hot seat' interview about one piece of their geography fieldwork (**PowerPoint 2**, slide 4). They should spend five minutes considering aims, methods, results, conclusions and evaluation. This task could be split into two with half the class looking at the physical fieldwork that the students have carried out, and half at the human fieldwork. This activity is a perfect AFL opportunity. Encourage students to suggest contributions to each group's interview: what did they miss?

PowerPoint 2, slide 5 provides raw data from bipolar surveys completed in Bristol's Temple Quarter (also on **Activity sheet 5**). Students can use this as an opportunity to develop ideas of types of data and data presentation techniques. Encourage students to think about these data – how could the data be presented? How could a correlation between distance from Temple Meads and quality of environment be tested? What are the weaknesses in the methods discussed?

Move on to the statistics quiz (a short summative assessment activity) on **PowerPoint 2**, slide 6/ **Activity sheet 6**. Go through the answers as a class (see slide 7), identifying any gaps in knowledge and understanding. Ask how students will fill these gaps then work through using notes, books and websites.

Consolidation
Finish the lesson with an activity to encourage students to think about how we collect data, present it and analyse it. Ask students, 'How could you statistically confirm whether house prices decrease with distance from the CBD in an urban area?' (**PowerPoint 2**, slide 8).

Lesson 2

Stimulus

Students may be asked questions about different approaches to data presentation in their exam. The simple 'match the graph to the name of the graph' activity on **PowerPoint 2**, slide 10 is intended to ensure students know what techniques they are using and what those techniques look like. Answers are provided on slide 11.

Development

Students review their RAG sheet from the last lesson - which areas do they need to focus on?

Students choose one of the four questions on **PowerPoint 2**, slide 13 to tackle, first underlining command words then circling subject terms and defining them. You will need to adapt slide 13 to show the number of marks for questions and how long students should spend on them as this varies between awarding organisations.

Students could structure their answer using PEE (point, explain, example; see slide 15), but if they feel confident in approaching the question in their own way this is fine, as PEE can be restrictive for some students. Sentence starters for one of the questions are suggested on slide 16, to support students who are struggling to answer or who need to answer in more detail.

Students should answer their chosen question, then swap answers to peer assess using the generic mark scheme on **PowerPoint 2**, slide 17. They can then answer another question.

The four questions students can choose from (**PowerPoint 2**, slide 13) are:

1 Draw an annotated sketch map to show the location and main features of the study area for your investigation.
2 Describe and justify one method of primary data collection used in your fieldwork.
3 Describe how you used one technique to analyse your data and outline the advantages of this technique.
4 Assess whether your fieldwork conclusions match the geographical theory, concept or idea on which your investigation was based.

Consolidation

Students should review their RAG rating again so they are aware of what they need to do to prepare for an assessment next lesson (**PowerPoint 2**, slide 18). This can be set as a home learning task.

Teaching tips

- Carrying out an activity and then reviewing it using a checklist helps students to focus on the key features. The checklist provided for the graphing activity can be used whenever students describe a graph.
- Time sensitive and group tasks can be a great way of injecting some fun and sense of challenge into revision tasks. Whole class tasks can also be a great way to raise the praise and let students know the excellent work they're all doing.

Lesson 3

Stimulus

A quick timed quiz on fieldwork - can the class answer all the questions on **PowerPoint 2**, slide 20 in 30 seconds? The faster each student answers their question, the more likely it is that the class will achieve its target. If the class does not achieve this within the time the activity could be repeated - and repeat answers are not allowed.

Development

Distribute a suitable exam question from the SAMs for your awarding organisation for your students to complete.

The students can then create a revision poster for this topic (**PowerPoint 2**, slides 22–23 or **Activity sheet 7**). This activity is deliberately positioned after the exam question. Exam questions can consequently be used as a diagnostic tool and to inform the students' revision posters. Remember that this is a revision scheme of learning, so all assessments are intended to provide students with an understanding of their own progress and ensure a more efficient and effective individual revision process.

Consolidation

Students should set themselves a home learning task (**PowerPoint 2**, slide 24). Based on the work they have done over the last three lessons, what else do students need to do to prepare for this element of the exam?

Geomorphic processes and landscape

Key questions

- Where are areas of highland and lowland located in the UK?
- How do weathering, erosion, transportation and deposition shape two distinct landscapes in the UK?
- How do these processes lead to the formation of distinctive landforms?
- How and why are UK landscapes managed?

Learning objectives

- To identify gaps in knowledge of geomorphic processes and landscape
- To reinforce key concepts and examples
- To practise extended answers for this topic
- To assess understanding of geomorphic processes and landscape

Resources

- Activity sheets
  8: Landform processes
  9: Revision poster
- PowerPoint
  3: Geomorphic processes and landscape

Lesson 1

Stimulus

Print a copy of the map on **PowerPoint 3**, slide 3 – A3-sized if possible. Stick this on the wall outside your classroom. Students get into groups of four and number themselves from 1 to 4. Ask all number 1 students to go out to look at the map for one minute. When the first student returns, they should draw what they remember from the map while the second student goes to look at the map for a minute. Continue until all four students have added to the map. Compare each group's map with the original map – which group's is the most accurate and complete?

Development

Students carry out a RAG-ing activity to identify areas of strength and areas for development by colour coding statements from the relevant specification, which you will need to provide (instructions on **PowerPoint 3**, slide 4). Students will refer back to this document several times, so it needs to be kept in a safe place.

Review processes of erosion, transportation and deposition (**PowerPoint 3**, slide 5). Can students think of an action to go with each process? Suggestions: hydraulic action – clapping; abrasion – tap palm with fist; attrition – tap both fists together. Follow your review of erosion up with a quick check on the difference between weathering and erosion (slide 6). Answers are given on slide 7.

Follow your review of erosion with a quick check on the difference between weathering and erosion (**PowerPoint 3**, slide 6).

Students will have studied two distinct UK landscapes: these could be river, coastal or glacial. Ask students which they studied, which landforms are associated with each landscape and how these landforms formed. Students complete the diagrams on **Activity sheet 8** to show how physical processes lead to the landforms in each landscape (this is modelled on **PowerPoint 3**, slide 9). For an extension task, ask students how these landforms are influenced by geology, climate and human activity.

Key examples of landscapes will have been used by students: ask them which locations they have used. Use Google Earth to zoom into each and then pose questions about the locations and their context (geology, climate, etc.).

Students choose two photographs of landforms from **PowerPoint 3**, slide 11 to sketch. Check that they have chosen landforms found in their two landscapes. They should add three annotations to each sketch to show how the landform formed. Remind the students that annotations are comments/ explanations, not just labels.

Students choose two photographs of landscapes from **PowerPoint 3**, slide 12 and answer the following questions: what evidence is there that these landscapes are being managed? Why do the landscapes need to be managed?

Consolidation

Finish the lesson with the UK physical landscape quick quiz on **PowerPoint 3**, slide 13. Answers are given on slide 14.

Lesson 2

Stimulus

Can students remember the processes of river/coastal erosion, transportation and deposition? Review the actions students came up with in Lesson 1 (**PowerPoint 3**, slide 16). Use questioning to check students' understanding of the processes and how they create different landforms.

Development

Students review their RAG sheet from the last lesson – which areas do they need to focus on?

Students choose one of the four questions on **PowerPoint 3**, slide 18 to tackle, first underlining command words and circling subject terms and defining them. You will need to adapt slide 18 to show the number of marks for questions and how long students should spend on them as this varies between awarding organisations.

Students could structure their answer using PEE (point, explain, example: **PowerPoint 3**, slide 20), but if they feel confident in approaching the question in their own way this is fine – PEE can be restrictive for some students.

Sentence starters are suggested on **PowerPoint 3**, slide 21 for one of the questions to support students who are struggling to answer or who need to answer in more detail.

Students should answer their chosen question, then swap answers with a peer and assess using the generic mark scheme on **PowerPoint 3**, slide 22. They can then answer another question.

Consolidation

Students should review their RAG rating again so they are aware of what they need to do to prepare for an assessment next lesson (**PowerPoint 3**, slide 23). This can be set as a home learning task.

Teaching tips

- Map from memory activities get students to look closely at the map/diagram and when they compare their map/diagram to the original, it highlights the need for accuracy.
- If students associate physical processes with the visual stimulus of an action they may recall them more easily (Paivio, 1971: theory of dual coding).
- Nuthall (2007) suggests that students need to 'experience at least three different sets of complete information about a concept before it is embedded in their network of knowledge.' It is therefore important to revisit concepts.
- The starter activity in lesson 3 includes the instruction to go back to any students who can't answer questions so that they can repeat the answer. This is inspired by Lemov's (2010) 'no opt out' which is a technique used to insist that all students answer questions.

Lesson 3

Stimulus

Give students time to think of a question about one of the UK landscapes they have studied (**PowerPoint 3**, slide 25). When you point at a student, they must stand up and ask their question, pointing in turn at another student who they would like to answer the question. That done, the second student then asks their question and selects someone to answer it. If a question isn't answered fully, the question-asker should pick someone else. Once a full answer has been received, the student(s) who couldn't answer fully should repeat the full answer.

Development

Students complete a revision poster for this topic (either creating their own or using the template on **PowerPoint 3**, slide 28, or **Activity Sheet 9**).

Provide a relevant exam question for students to answer from the SAM for your awarding organisation. Take the answers in to mark yourself, giving feedback about areas of strength and areas for improvement. Students should be given time to improve their answer after receiving feedback.

Consolidation

Students should set themselves a home learning task (**PowerPoint 3**, slide 29). Based on the work they have done over the last three lessons, what else do they need to do to prepare for this element of the exam?

Changing weather and climate

Key questions
- What are the causes and consequences of and responses to extreme weather conditions and hazards?
- How can real world examples of weather hazards be described and explained?
- How does the global circulation system influence weather and climate?
- How is climate change caused by both human and physical processes?

Learning objectives
- To identify gaps in knowledge of changing weather and climate
- To reinforce key concepts and examples
- To practise extended answers for this topic
- To assess understanding of changing weather and climate

Resources
- Activity sheets
  - 10: The global circulation system
  - 11: Describing change
  - 12: Revision poster
- PowerPoint
  - 4: Changing weather and climate

Lesson 1

Stimulus
Using **PowerPoint 4**, slide 2, slowly remove the shapes from the picture, asking students to guess the weather hazard (the photograph shows a satellite image of a tropical storm).

Development
Students carry out a RAG-ing activity to identify areas of strength and areas for development by colour coding statements from the relevant specification, which you will need to provide (instructions on **PowerPoint 4**, slide 3). Students will refer back to this document several times so it needs to be kept in a safe place.

Give students two minutes to look at the diagram of the global circulation system (**Activity sheet 10** or **PowerPoint 4**, slide 4), then ask one student to come to the front of the room to take the 'hot seat'. You can ask them the questions from **PowerPoint 4**, slide 5 (these are also included on **Activity sheet 10**, page 2), and/or come up with questions of your own. If the student gets stuck, you could let them choose another student to help them. Answers are provided on slide 6.

Read the class the story of a storm from **PowerPoint 4**, slide 7. Ask them to talk in pairs to finish the story, then work individually to write a story for the storm hazard they have studied, including causes, consequences and responses. Share some of the stories and discuss points included and omitted.

Look at the images on **PowerPoint 4**, slide 8. How is each linked to causes of climate change? Draw out student answers using questioning. Discuss which causes are the most significant.

Study the graph showing changes in atmospheric carbon dioxide over time (**PowerPoint 4**, slide 9 or **Activity sheet 11**). Students write a paragraph describing the changes shown. Students use the checklist provided to improve their answers.

Consolidation
Finish the lesson with the true or false quiz on **PowerPoint 4**, slide 10. Answers are provided on slide 11.

Lesson 2

Stimulus

Students work in pairs to draw the global circulation system on balloons, paper plates or paper. Peer assess against criteria shown on **PowerPoint 4**, slide 13.

Development

Students review their RAG sheet from the last lesson - which areas do they need to focus on?

Students choose one of the four questions on **PowerPoint 4**, slide 15 to tackle, first underlining command words and circling subject terms and defining them. You will need to adapt slide 15 to show the number of marks for questions and how long students should spend on them as this varies between awarding organisations.

Students could structure their answer using PEE (point, explain, example: **PowerPoint 4**, slide 17), but if they feel confident in approaching the question in their own way this is fine as PEE can be restrictive for some students.

Sentence starters are suggested (on **PowerPoint 4**, slide 18) for one of the questions to support students who are struggling to answer or who need to answer in more detail.

Students should answer their chosen question, then swap answers with a peer and assess using the generic mark scheme on **PowerPoint 4**, slide 19. They can then answer another question.

Consolidation

Students should review their RAG rating again so they are aware of what they need to do to prepare for an assessment next lesson (**PowerPoint 4**, slide 20). This can be set as a home learning task.

Teaching tips

- Carrying out an activity and then reviewing it using a checklist helps students to focus on the key features.
- Drawing on a balloon or paper plate can be used whenever students need to know a global pattern. It encourages students to pay attention to detail as they are presenting the information in a different way; hopefully this activity will also be memorable. Board pens can also be used to draw on many school tables, allowing students to construct large mind maps, etc.
- Nuthall (2007) says that activities should be designed so that students can't avoid taking part in them, otherwise they miss out on opportunities to learn. Activities such as explaining the causes of a weather hazard by everyone in the class saying one word each mean that all students are involved.

Lesson 3

Stimulus

Choose a weather hazard, such as a tropical storm. Explain the causes of the hazard as a class, with each person contributing one word to the explanation (see **PowerPoint 4**, slide 22).

Development

Provide a relevant exam question for students to answer from the SAM for your awarding organisation. Take the answers in to mark yourself, giving feedback about areas of strength and areas for improvement. Students should be given time to improve their answer after receiving feedback. There is an additional extended exam question on **PowerPoint 4**, slide 23.

Students complete a revision poster for this topic, either creating their own or using the template on **PowerPoint 4**, slide 25, or **Activity sheet 12**.

Consolidation

Students should set themselves a home learning task (**PowerPoint 4**, slide 26). Based on the work they have done over the last three lessons, what else do they need to do to prepare for this element of the exam?

Global ecosystems and biodiversity

Key questions

- What are the characteristics of large-scale natural global ecosystems and how are they distributed?
- How are climate, soil, water, plants, animals and humans interdependent in two ecosystems?
- How are ecosystems used unsustainably and sustainably?

Learning objectives

- To identify gaps in knowledge of global ecosystems and biodiversity
- To reinforce key concepts and examples
- To practise extended answers for this topic
- To assess understanding of global ecosystems and biodiversity

Resources

- Activity sheets
  13: Ecosystem diagrams
  14: Revision poster
- PowerPoint
  5: Global ecosystems and biodiversity

Lesson 1

Stimulus

Students look at images of different large-scale natural global ecosystems (**PowerPoint 5**, slide 2) in groups, deciding what the characteristics of each ecosystem are and where each would be found in the world. Groups then share their ideas with the class.

Development

Students carry out a RAG-ing activity to identify areas of strength and areas for development by colour coding statements from the relevant specification, which you will need to provide (instructions on **PowerPoint 5**, slide 3). Students will refer back to this document several times so it needs to be kept in a safe place.

Students will have studied two ecosystems: ask them which ones they have studied then use Google Earth to zoom into each and discuss them. Students produce a diagram for each ecosystem studied to show how the climate, soil, water, plants, animals and humans are interdependent (**PowerPoint 5**, slide 5 or **Activity sheet 12**). Use atlases/textbooks/websites to support points with useful facts and figures, e.g. average temperature, annual rainfall. This is a concept mapping activity – the most important aspect is the links made between each component and these should be fully explained. An example for the Sahara Desert is provided on slide 6. You could challenge students to develop their explanations of links using the 'Why, why, why?' technique – ask them to read their explanation, then keep asking them 'Why?' until the link is *fully* explained.

The ecosystems studied can be used in both sustainable and unsustainable ways. Students complete a table to show examples using the template shown on **PowerPoint 5**, slide 7. These may relate to living in the ecosystem, farming in it, use by multinational companies, tourism, energy production or other uses.

Consolidation

Undertake the food web challenge (see **PowerPoint 5**, slide 8). Choose one of the ecosystems studied. Each student writes the name of a component from this ecosystem on a piece of paper (make sure students choose different components – you may wish to prepare some back up examples in case of too much duplication). Students stand in a circle. Give one student a ball of string – they should keep hold of the end and pass the ball to another student whose component is linked to theirs in the food web. Continue this to create a food web. Choose one student to drop the string – which other components does this affect? Why is this important?

Lesson 2

Stimulus
Complete the 'Would you rather...?' exercise on **PowerPoint 5**, slide 10. Students must justify their choices with reference to the ecosystems stated. An example answer is provided on slide 11.

Development
Students review their RAG sheet from the last lesson - which areas do they need to focus on?

Students choose one of the four questions on **PowerPoint 5**, slide 13 to tackle, first underlining command words and circling subject terms and defining them. You will need to adapt slide 13 to show the number of marks for questions and how long students should spend on them as this varies between awarding organisations.

Students could structure their answer using PEE (point, explain, example: **PowerPoint 5**, slide 15), but if they feel confident in approaching the question in their own way this is fine - PEE can be restrictive for some students.

Sentence starters are suggested (on **PowerPoint 5**, slide 16) for one of the questions to support students who are struggling to answer or who need to answer in more detail.

Students should answer their chosen question, then swap answers with a peer and assess using the generic mark scheme on slide 17. They can then answer another question.

Consolidation
Students should review their RAG rating again so they are aware of what they need to do to prepare for an assessment next lesson (**PowerPoint 5**, slide 18). This can be set as a home learning task.

Teaching tips
- As well as using Google Earth and video clips, consider using Google Expeditions to explore your chosen ecosystems.
- Teachers can bring ecosystems into their classrooms by using plants or foods. For example, if you are studying deserts, bring in a cactus and discuss how it has adapted to the desert ecosystem, or dates for students to eat. Activities that make concepts more tangible may be particularly helpful for low prior achievers.
- Use of place specific detail to develop points is key to success in GCSE geography. Use questioning to draw out specific details related to the ecosystems' climates, vegetation, animals, etc.

Lesson 3

Stimulus
Watch a clip of one or both of the ecosystems studied. Ask students to note the 5Ws for the clip: What, where, when, who, why? (see **PowerPoint 5**, slide 20).

Development
Provide a relevant exam question for students to answer from the SAM for your awarding organisation. Take the answers in to mark yourself, giving feedback about areas of strength and areas for improvement. Students should be given time to improve their answer after receiving feedback.

Students complete a revision poster for this topic (either creating their own or using the template on **PowerPoint 5**, slide 23, or **Activity sheet 14**).

Consolidation
Students should set themselves a home learning task (**PowerPoint 5**, slide 24). Based on the work they have done over the last three lessons, what else do students need to do to prepare for this element of the exam?

Resources and their management

Key questions

- What are natural resources?
- How can resource exploitation have an impact on people and the environment?
- How has supply and demand for natural resources changed?

Learning objectives

- To identify gaps in knowledge of resources and their management
- To reinforce key concepts and examples
- To practise extended answers for this topic
- To assess understanding of resources and their management

Resources

- Activity sheets
  15: Energy mix
  16: Mix and match
  17: Revision poster
- PowerPoint
  6: Resources and their management

Lesson 1

Stimulus

Ask the students what resources have they used so far today. This activity can be developed into a concept map activity based on food, energy and water resources. Students should then consider the image of a child from a LIC (**PowerPoint 6**, slide 2). Develop from this stimulus: how is this child's resource usage likely to be different from ours? Why? How does this relate to well-being?

Development

Students carry out a RAG-ing activity to identify areas of strength and areas for development by colour coding statements from the relevant specification, which you will need to provide (instructions on **PowerPoint 6**, slide 3). Students will refer back to this document several times, so it needs to be kept in a safe place.

The excellent work of www.gapminder.org is a great way to explore geographical issues in a powerfully visual way. When exploring consumption and production of resources these graphs can really develop students' comparison of multiple pieces of information. For example, ask students to analyse energy use per person and energy production per person over time (**PowerPoint 6**, slide 4).

Students should look at one resource issue in more detail. Choose the relevant sections from the activities below:

Focus on food:

- Encourage students to look at the images of food on **PowerPoint 6**, slide 5 or real examples and for each answer these questions: When are these available to buy in the UK? When are they in season in the UK? Where do they come from when not in season? This will highlight the global nature of food supply and can also start to develop ideas of food miles and climate change.
- Students then draw up a cost/ benefit analysis for buying one of the food items out of season (**PowerPoint 6**, slide 5). They should consider aspects such as freshness, food miles, impact on local and national economies, etc. Are the benefits worth the costs?
- How can food production be more sustainable? Students can look at the images on **PowerPoint 6**, slide 6 for ideas.

Focus on water:

- Students consider the images on **PowerPoint 6**, slide 7: how can access to safe water affect a person's well-being? Why can access be different in different places?
- What affects how much water is available in a place and how much is consumed? Students draw a flow diagram to show this, including factors such as economic development, population growth, climate, geology, pollution and infrastructure (**PowerPoint 6**, slide 8). Make sure students write a description of how each factor affects demand or supply alongside the arrow.
- How can water supplies be managed more sustainably? Students should use the keywords on **PowerPoint 6**, slide 9 in their answers.

Focus on energy:

- **PowerPoint 6**, slide 10 and **Activity sheet 15** show a pie chart of the US energy mix in

Teaching tips

- www.gapminder.org has a huge number useful graphs that can be used not only for resources but also to demonstrate a range of geographical issues that are relevant to all levels.
- If you have a department Twitter account you could tweet photographs of the results of tasks such as mix and match activity. You could also post links to websites and ideas for revision.
- Be wary of older textbooks that are unlikely to include the most up to date information about, for example, energy consumption per household decreasing.

2015. Students could work through the following questions in pairs: a) Describe the US's energy mix in 2015; b) Suggest *how* the US's energy mix is likely to change in the future; c) Explain *why* the US's energy mix is likely to change in the future.

- Divide different energy resources between groups (see **PowerPoint 6**, slide 11). Each group should consider the economic and environmental issues associated with the exploitation of their given resource. The groups should then summarise each resource in 140 characters and feed back to the class.
- How can energy resources be managed more sustainably? Students can use the images on **PowerPoint 6**, slide 12 for ideas.

Consolidation

Why might people have a different opinion on whether an energy resource should be exploited depending on whether they are looking at it from a local or national perspective (**PowerPoint 6**, slide 13)? If students are struggling to answer this question, get them to think about a specific energy source, e.g. a wind farm. Why might local people have a more negative perception of wind energy than people who live away from wind farms?

Lesson 2

Stimulus

Ask students: 'If you had the power to provide everyone in the world with food **or** water **or** energy, which one would you choose? Why?' (**PowerPoint 6**, slide 15). This activity could be conducted with students moving to a corner of the room that represents their chosen resource and then justifying why they have stood there.

Development

Students review their RAG sheet from the last lesson - which areas do they need to focus on?

Students choose one of the four questions on **PowerPoint 6**, slide 17 to tackle, first underlining command words and circling subject terms and defining them. You will need to adapt slide 17 to show the number of marks for questions and how long students should spend on them as this varies between awarding organisations.

Students could structure their answer using PEE (point, explain, example: **PowerPoint 6**, slide 19), but if they feel confident in approaching the question in their own way this is fine as PEE can be restrictive for some students.

Sentence starters are suggested on **PowerPoint 6**, slide 20 for one of the questions to support students who are struggling to answer or who need to answer in more detail.

Students should answer their chosen question, then swap answers with a peer and assess using the generic mark scheme on **PowerPoint 6**, slide 21. They can then answer another question.

Consolidation

Students should review their RAG rating again so they are aware of what they need to do to prepare for an assessment next lesson (**PowerPoint 6**, slide 22). This can be set as a home learning task.

Lesson 3

Stimulus

The simple mix and match key terms and definitions activity on **PowerPoint 6**, slide 24 or **Activity sheet 16** can be extended with students being asked to add their own contribution of a key term and definition. Answers are provided on slide 25.

Development

Provide a relevant exam question for students to answer from the SAM for your awarding organisation (an additional exam question is provided on **PowerPoint 6**, slide 26). Take the answers in to mark yourself, giving feedback about areas of strength and areas for improvement. Students should be given time to improve their answer after receiving feedback.

Students complete a revision poster for this topic (either creating their own or using the template on **PowerPoint 6**, slide 28 or **Activity sheet 17**).

Consolidation

Students should set themselves a home learning task (**PowerPoint 6**, slide 29). Based on the work they have done over the last three lessons, what else do they need to do to prepare for this element of the exam?

Cities and urban society

Key questions

- What are the causes and effects of rapid urbanisation and contrasting urban trends in different parts of the world?
- What is life like in two cities in two contrasting countries?
- What are the contemporary challenges arising from and influencing urban change in each city?

Learning objectives

- To identify gaps in knowledge of cities and urban society
- To reinforce key concepts and examples
- To practise extended answers for this topic
- To assess understanding of cities and urban society

Resources

- Activity sheets
  18: City concept map
  19: Migrant stories
  20: Revision poster
- PowerPoint
  7: Cities and urban society

Lesson 1

Stimulus

Students look at the images on **PowerPoint 7**, slide 2 and consider how these factors cause urbanisation. How could they be categorised? Encourage students to consider categories such as social and environmental factors. Details about each photo are provided on slide 3.

Development

Students carry out a RAG-ing activity to identify areas of strength and areas for development by colour coding statements from the relevant specification, which you will need to provide (instructions on **PowerPoint 7**, slide 4). Students will refer back to this document several times so it needs to be kept in a safe place.

Remind students of the two cities they have studied then use Google Earth to zoom into each and pose questions about the locations and their context (**PowerPoint 7**, slide 5).

Challenge students to summarise the two cities studied in four facts, three sentences, two words and one emotion (**PowerPoint 7**, slide 6), then share ideas as a class. Use questioning to deepen understanding and tackle misconceptions, for example asking, 'Can you support that fact with evidence?'

Students produce two concept maps on factors influencing change for both cities. Students could create their own format or use the template on **PowerPoint 7**, slide 7 or **Activity sheet 18**. (A concept map using the example of Kampala in Uganda has been provided on **PowerPoint 7**, slide 8). The aim is to summarise each case study on one sheet for easy revision, so stress the need to present this work carefully and ensure it is informative. This task will take some time, so may need to be finished at home.

Students read the migrant story (**PowerPoint 7**, slides 9 and 10 or **Activity sheet 19**). Discuss which of the cities they have studied the stories might relate to, and the push and pull factors involved in each decision. What challenges might these migrations present and how are these challenges being tackled? Encourage students to use appropriate geographical terminology during these discussions.

Consolidation

Write 12 keywords from this topic on the board. Students draw a 3x3 grid and add a keyword into each grid square (modelled on **PowerPoint 7**, slide 11). The teacher then calls out and defines the keywords in a random order, while students check off the words on their grid until someone gets a line, then a full house.

Lesson 2

Stimulus

Students study **PowerPoint 7**, slide 13, and work out which word is the odd one out in each row. Some students may come up with their own odd one out. Use questioning to check understanding, asking targeted students which they think is the odd one out and why. Answers are on slide 14.

Development

Students review their RAG sheet from the last lesson – which areas do they need to focus on?

Students choose one of the four questions on **PowerPoint 7**, slide 16 to tackle, first underlining command words and circling subject terms and defining them. You will need to adapt slide 16 to show the number of marks for questions and how long students should spend on them as this varies between awarding organisations.

Students could structure their answer using PEE (point, explain, example: **PowerPoint 7**, slide 18), but if they feel confident in approaching the question in their own way this is fine as PEE can be restrictive for some students.

Sentence starters are suggested (on **PowerPoint 7**, slide 19) for one of the questions to support students who are struggling to answer or who need to answer in more detail.

Students should answer their chosen question, then swap answers with a peer and assess using the generic mark scheme on **PowerPoint 7**, slide 20. They can then answer another question.

Consolidation

Students should review their RAG rating again so they are aware of what they need to do to prepare for an assessment next lesson (**PowerPoint 7**, slide 21). This can be set as a home learning task.

Lesson 3

Stimulus

Students choose one of the cities they have studied and consider why it is important for its region, country and the wider world (**PowerPoint 7**, slide 23). Encourage students to share their thoughts and draw out understanding using questioning.

Development

Provide a relevant exam question for students to answer from the SAM for your awarding organisation (There is an additional exam question on **PowerPoint 7**, slide 24). Take the answers in to mark yourself, giving feedback about areas of strength and areas for improvement. Students should be given time to improve their answer after receiving feedback.

Students complete a revision poster for this topic (either creating their own or using the template on **PowerPoint 7**, slides 25–26 or **Activity sheet 20**). Some boxes have been left without titles to allow you to customise the template according to the requirements of your specification.

Consolidation

Students should set themselves a home learning task (**PowerPoint 7**, slide 27). Based on the work they have done over the last three lessons, what else do students need to do to prepare for this element of the exam?

Teaching tips

- Students need to use the notes they made when they first studied this topic, as revision books will often have different case studies. Share links to useful resources about their cities.
- Be ready to tackle any misconceptions that may arise about the cities studied and about migration. It is important that students can support their statements with evidence.
- It is important to make it clear when answers are right. Lemov (2010) suggests only telling a student that their answer is right when the entire answer you are looking for is given.

Global economic and development issues

Key questions

- What do we mean by the term development?
- How uneven is the pattern of development and how has it changed over time?
- What are the impacts and solutions to uneven patterns of development?

Learning objectives

- To identify gaps in knowledge of global economic and development issues
- To reinforce key concepts and examples
- To practise extended answers for this topic
- To assess understanding of global economic and development issues

Resources

- Activity sheets
  21: Development indicators
  22: Revision poster
- PowerPoint
  8: Global economic and development issues

Lesson 1

Stimulus

Students match the images to the key terms on **PowerPoint 8**, slide 2 (answers are provided on slide 3). Ask students to discuss their thought processes while completing this task: what is it about the images and their understanding of the key terms that makes the link in each case?

Development

Students carry out a RAG-ing activity to identify areas of strength and areas for development by colour coding statements from the relevant specification, which you will need to provide (instructions on **PowerPoint 8**, slide 4). Students will refer back to this document several times so it needs to be kept in a safe place.

Students study the initials on **PowerPoint 8**, slide 5. Which development indicators do they refer to? (answers are provided on slide 6) Can they be categorised into social and economic? Are some more useful than others? Why?

Students look at the images **PowerPoint 8**, slide 7 - how are these related to causes of uneven development? Can they be categorised into physical, economic and historical causes? (answers are provided on slide 8)

Students will have studied a low income country (LIC) or new emerging economy (NEE). Which country have they studied? Use Google Earth or similar to zoom in and discuss the country's location. What is the wider political, social and environmental context within which the country is placed? Students produce a sketchnote to show this: an example is provided on **PowerPoint 8**, slide 9.

What are the key industries and areas for investment in the country studied? How is this changing over time (**PowerPoint 8**, slide 10)? Students write a paragraph to explore this, then peer assess and improve.

Consolidation

Can development be divided into inputs and outputs? This task is an attempt to produce a simple model for the purpose of revision. Ask students to highlight the inputs that affect the level of development in your case study country and the outputs or consequences this level of development may have (**PowerPoint 8**, slide 11). After this it may be worth discussing with the class why, in real life, it is not as simple as inputs and outputs and how complex geographical interrelationships can impact on a country's development in ways that cannot always be predicted.

Lesson 2

Stimulus

Students complete a quiz (**PowerPoint 8**, slide 13) to review their case study country. You may wish to add an answers slide to the PowerPoint to allow students to self or peer assess.

Development

Students review their RAG sheet from the last lesson – which areas do they need to focus on?

Students choose one of the four questions on **PowerPoint 8**, slide 15 to tackle, first underlining command words and circling subject terms and defining them. You will need to adapt slide 15 to show the number of marks for questions and how long students should spend on them as this varies between awarding organisations.

Students could structure their answer using PEE (point, explain, example: **PowerPoint 8**, slide 17), but if they feel confident in approaching the question in their own way this is fine as PEE can be restrictive for some students.

Sentence starters are suggested (on **PowerPoint 8**, slide 18) for one of the questions to support students who are struggling to answer or who need to answer in more detail.

Students should answer their chosen question, then swap answers with a peer and assess using the generic mark scheme on slide 19. They can then answer another question.

Consolidation

Students should review their RAG rating so that they know what they need to do to prepare for an assessment next lesson (**PowerPoint 8**, slide 20). This can be set as a home learning task.

Lesson 3

Stimulus

Students should look at the development indicator cards for three of the countries on **PowerPoint 8**, slide 22 or **Activity sheet 21**. What does this information tell us about the relative development of these countries? What are the limitations of these indicators?

Development

Provide a relevant exam question for students to answer from the SAM for your awarding organisation (There is an additional exam question on **PowerPoint 8**, slide 23). Take the answers in to mark yourself, giving feedback about areas of strength and areas for improvement. Students should be given time to improve their answer after receiving feedback.

Students complete a revision poster for this topic (either creating their own or using the template on **PowerPoint 8**, slide 25 or **Activity sheet 22**).

Consolidation

Students should set themselves a home learning task (**PowerPoint 8**, slide 26). Based on the work they have done over the last three lessons, what else do students need to do to prepare for this element of the exam?

Teaching tips

- This topic has a huge amount of potential to engage students with some complex ideas and geographical processes. Use the opportunity to stretch level 9 students.
- The activities in this lesson could be complemented by playing the Gapminder card game (https://www.gapminder.org/downloads/card-game).
- There are also many resources to be found on the Geographical Association website: www.geography.org.uk – search for the country or issue that you are interested in.
- Be ready to tackle any misconceptions that may arise about development issues. It is important that students can support their analysis with evidence.
- Lemov (2010) suggests that multiple takes (e.g. explaining something in three different ways) can encourage fluency of use of subject specific terminology.

Tectonic hazards

Key questions

- How do physical processes cause earthquakes and volcanic eruptions?
- What are the effects of, and responses to, a tectonic hazard and how they can vary between areas of contrasting levels of wealth?
- How can management reduce the effects of a tectonic hazard?

Learning objectives

- To identify gaps in knowledge of tectonic hazards
- To reinforce key concepts and examples
- To practise extended answers for this topic
- To assess understanding of tectonic hazards

Resources

- Activity sheets
  23: Fact file
  24: Revision poster
- PowerPoint
  9: Tectonic hazards

Lesson 1

Stimulus

Students work in groups to create a model to show what happens at one type of plate margin, using items found in the classroom - pencil cases, books, etc. (**PowerPoint 9**, slide 2) The class should share their ideas; discuss these and tackle any misconceptions.

Development

Students carry out a RAG-ing activity to identify areas of strength and areas for development by colour coding statements from the relevant specification, which you will need to provide (instructions on **PowerPoint 9**, slide 3). Students will refer back to this document several times so it needs to be kept in a safe place.

Using www.geolsoc.org.uk/Plate-Tectonics (**PowerPoint 9**, slide 4) students describe and explain the distribution of volcanoes and earthquakes by clicking on the different options for the map. They can use the 'pioneers of plate tectonics' tab to find out about plate tectonic theory and the 'plate margins' tab to explore the different types of margin. Make sure that the students look at the section about how plates move to check that they are aware of the influences of both convection currents and slab pull. There are 'test your knowledge' activities that students could complete; these could be done as a class, individually or for home learning.

Students will have studied at least one example of a tectonic hazard. Ask them what their example is and where it is located. Use Google Earth or similar to zoom in and discuss the location and its context (**PowerPoint 9**, slide 5).

Students complete a fact file for their example of a tectonic hazard, including information about causes, consequences, responses and the level of development of the location (**PowerPoint 9**, slide 6 or **Activity sheet 23**). If they have studied more than one example they could complete additional fact files.

Consolidation

Ask whether students would rather experience a tectonic hazard in a lower or higher income country. Why? (**PowerPoint 9**, slide 7). Draw out thoughts using questioning to look at aspects such as how people prepare for hazards in higher income countries, the role of insurance in sharing risk, provision of emergency services, available technology, etc.

This topic is not included in the GCSE core content, but is included in most GCSE geography specifications. Check your specification to see its requirements for this topic.

Lesson 2

Stimulus

Put a chain slightly over the edge of a table. Pull it so that more overhangs - eventually it will start to move off the table due to the weight of chain that is no longer supported by the table. How does this relate to slab pull? This activity could be carried out by the teacher as a demonstration or by groups of students if several lengths of chain are available.

Development

Students review their RAG sheet from the last lesson - which areas do they need to focus on?

Students choose one of the four questions on **PowerPoint 9**, slide 10 to tackle, first underlining command words and circling subject terms and defining them. You will need to adapt slide 10 to show the number of marks for questions and how long students should spend on them as this varies between awarding organisations.

Students could structure their answer using PEE (point, explain, example: **PowerPoint 9**, slide 12), but if they feel confident in approaching the question in their own way this is fine as PEE can be restrictive for some students.

Sentence starters are suggested (on **PowerPoint 9**, slide 13) for one of the questions to support students who are struggling to answer or who need to answer in more detail.

Students should answer their chosen question, then swap answers with a peer and assess using the generic mark scheme on slide 14. They can then answer another question.

Consolidation

Students should review their RAG rating again so that they know what they need to do to prepare for an assessment next lesson (**PowerPoint 9**, slide 15). This can be set as a home learning task.

Teaching tips

- Take photos of the students' plate margin models - students could annotate these and stick them in their notes as revision reminders.
- Use a departmental Twitter account to post links to websites and ideas for revision.
- www.geolsoc.org.uk/Plate-Tectonics is an excellent website to use as it is up to date - be wary of older textbooks that are unlikely to include elements such as slab pull and ridge push.

Lesson 3

Stimulus

Students look at the images from Iceland from **PowerPoint 9**, slide 17 and use them as prompts to think of the potential costs and benefits of living in an area that is tectonically active. Students use think, pair, share to explore this question.

Development

Provide a relevant exam question for students to answer from the SAM for your awarding organisation (There is an additional exam question on **PowerPoint 9**, slide 18). Take the answers in to mark yourself, giving feedback about areas of strength and areas for improvement. Students should be given time to improve their answer after receiving feedback.

Students complete a revision poster for this topic (either creating their own or using the template on **PowerPoint 9**, slides 19-20 or **Activity sheet 24**).

Consolidation

Students should then set themselves a home learning task (**PowerPoint 9**, slide 21). Based on the work they have done over the last three lessons, what else do students need to do to prepare for this element of the exam?

Case studies

Key questions

- What are the key case studies we have studied?
- How do case studies link to the broader issues we have studied?
- What are the key physical and human features of our case studies?

Learning objectives

- To identify gaps in knowledge of case studies
- To reinforce key concepts and examples
- To practise extended answers for this topic
- To assess understanding of case studies

Resources

- Activity sheets
  25: Case study card
  26: Improve the answer
  27: Revision poster
- PowerPoint
  10: Case studies

Lesson 1

Stimulus

Which case studies have students studied? They have already revised these in recent lessons, so should be able to come up with a quick list. Why are these case studies so important? (**PowerPoint 10**, slide 2)

Development

Students carry out a RAG-ing activity to identify areas of strength and areas for development by colour coding statements from the relevant specification, which you will need to provide (instructions on **PowerPoint 10**, slide 3). Students will refer back to this document several times so it needs to be kept in a safe place.

Students work in groups to produce a revision resource for one case study using their own notes, textbooks, etc. They could produce this in a variety of ways (see **PowerPoint 10**, slide 4) but need to ensure that they include key terms and facts and important human and physical features and how they interact. Since the aim is to cover all case studies, you will need to allocate specific case studies to each group.

Resources produced can be shared either by using them in a carousel or by groups presenting them to the class. As the resources are shared, students should produce a case study card as shown on **PowerPoint 10**, slide 6 (also available on **Activity sheet 25**). By the end of the activity, students should have cards for each of their case studies.

Consolidation

Work with the class to identify the strengths of revision resources produced. Do any need further development?

Lesson 2

Stimulus

Students read the exemplar answer to the question on **PowerPoint 10**, slide 8 (also on **Activity sheet 26**). How could this answer be improved by using the case study more effectively? Students should annotate the answer to indicate where place-specific detail could be added to improve the answer. For example, where the answer says 'Tourists might also visit', students could annotate to say 'Add place-specific detail here about specific tourism opportunities from your desert case study'.

Development

Students review their RAG sheet from the last lesson - which areas do they need to focus on?

Students choose one of the four questions on **PowerPoint 10**, slide 10 to tackle, first underlining command words and circling subject terms and defining them. You will need to adapt slide 10 to show the number of marks for questions and how long students should spend on them as this varies between awarding organisations.

Students could structure their answer using PEE (point, explain, example: **PowerPoint 10**, slide 12), but if they feel confident in approaching the question in their own way this is fine as PEE can be restrictive for some students.

Sentence starters are suggested (on **PowerPoint 10**, slide 13) for one of the questions to support students who are struggling to answer or who need to answer in more detail. Students should answer their chosen question, then swap answers with a peer and assess using the generic mark scheme on slide 14. They can then answer another question.

Consolidation

Students should review their RAG rating again so they are aware of what they need to do to prepare for an assessment next lesson (**PowerPoint 10**, slide 15). This can be set as a home learning task.

Teaching tips

- Check your specification for its use of case studies and examples. Students are expected to know case studies in much more detail than examples, so make sure students are clear on which are which.
- These lessons are planned to come at the end of the revision scheme of learning. They enable the students to revisit topics revised previously through the case studies. Teachers will have marked exam answers on the different topics and so will be able to tweak this lesson to ensure it tackles any misconceptions or areas of weakness identified.
- The activities are planned to be more independent as by this stage students should be fully focused on their exams and ready to take on this level of responsibility.

Lesson 3

(This lesson is optional as it may have already been covered in previous lessons.)

Stimulus

Discuss with the class when it is a good idea to refer to a case study in an exam (**PowerPoint 10**, slide 17). Make it clear to students that it is essential that they use case studies when they are asked to in the question, but it is also a good idea to use them to support answers to other extended questions.

Development

Provide a relevant exam question for students to answer from the SAM for your awarding organisation. Take the answers in to mark yourself, giving feedback about areas of strength and areas for improvement. Students should be given time to improve their answer after receiving feedback.

Students complete a revision poster for this topic (either creating their own or using the template on **PowerPoint 10**, slides 19-20 or **Activity sheet 27**).

Consolidation

Students should set themselves a home learning task (**PowerPoint 10**, slide 21). Based on the work they have done over the last three lessons, what else do students need to do to prepare for this element of the exam?

Further teaching ideas

As a revision resource this Toolkit contains a broad range of pedagogical techniques used to review knowledge and build understanding. This section provides a range of further teaching ideas that can be used in addition to the ones already demonstrated. Many of the ideas on these pages are based on the work of Doug Lemov (2010) and Jim Smith (2017) and build on their ideas of pragmatic, student-focused classroom activities.

Revision ideas

Only ask once

In order to support a sense of ownership and shared progress when it comes to the learning taking place within your classroom, encourage students to never ask the same question more than once. Before students ask a question, they should come to the desk and take a sticky note to write the question on; once the question is answered, the student writes the answer on the sticky note then sticks it back on the desk. The next time a student has a question they must check all the completed sticky notes to see if it has already been asked/answered. This technique encourages and formalises students learning from their peers.

Stretch it

Prepare a series of follow-up questions that will always be asked when a student answers a question. Questions such as 'Why is that important?' or 'How does that link to something else we have studied?' will encourage students to extend their thinking and ensure that the expectation is in place that students should always go the extra mile when analysing key concepts.

Geoguessr.com

GeoGuessr is a web-based geographic discovery game that uses a semi-randomised Google Street View location and requires players to guess their location in the world using only the clues visible. It could be used with students to explore anything from climate and ecosystems to development geography. The visual information the students are receiving and interpreting is rich and students should be encouraged to ensure that their geographical understanding is clear by using key terms and facts to support their processing.

Google Expeditions

Google Expeditions is an excellent VR app that can be used on tablets or phones as well as VR headsets. It allows students to investigate places that they would never be able to visit in a regular school day – from Mumbai to the Great Barrier Reef. Last year we held a Google Expedition day, and being able to explore Nepal after the earthquake really helped our students flesh out their case study.

Revision rapping

We have worked for a number of years with a hip-hop education company called Class of Poets. The rapper Silas Zephania works with our students to develop revision raps that highlight key terms and facts for topics and strings them all together with a beat that will ensure the students leave rapping all their favourite key geographical terminology. When we use this activity in school we often combine it with a grid that we ask the students to populate with key terms and key facts and this is used as a support tool for the students to create their revision rap.

Entry routine and do now

This is taken straight from the pages of Lemov's *Teach like a Champion*. If an activity requires an information pack or specific resources, ensure students know to collect them on their way to their seat and that the first task is shown on the board so that students can begin as soon as they sit down. This encourages students to be autonomous in their pursuit of learning and provides you with an opportunity to stand back and provide support rather than driving the administration of the activity.

What's on your head?

This is a paired activity where each student in the pair writes a key term onto a sticky note. The note is then stuck onto their partner's forehead. Each person must try to guess the key term stuck to their head by asking questions; their partner is not allowed to say (or spell) the word.

Simple to complex

Show students two lists of questions: one must be a list of simple questions and one must be a list of more complex and analytical questions. Students must choose a question from each and also identify why the complex question is different from the simple. It is important to encourage students to develop metacognition so that they understand what it is they are doing and what it is they need to do.

21

As per standard rules of 21, in a group (of five or more) you count to 21 in a clockwise direction. If the person before you says two numbers the direction reverses; if the person before you says three numbers it skips you; if you are the person that says 21 then you lose and you must change one of the numbers so that instead of saying that number your fellow players will have to say a geographical key term, e.g. one... two... primary impact... four. This continues until all the numbers are replaced with key geographical terms or facts.

Prior knowledge

Ed Hirsch points out that prior knowledge is one of the most significant contributing factors when it comes to comprehension. Produce a prior knowledge document that could prove useful in exploring topics, then display this on students' desks so that they can use it when answering questions later in the lesson.

Homework ideas

Knowledge organisers

Students summarise a topic in 20 key ideas or facts that they will have to revise in advance of a test or assessment.

Geog your memory

Students must set themselves five key questions that they need to answer for homework. The questions must be linked to the RAG rating activity that they have already completed.

Podcaster

Encourage students to use simple audio recorders on phones or tablets to record an informative revision podcast. Encourage students to work in groups and focus on small sections of a topic and on what they would want and need to know the week before the exam. These can then be shared to create a whole class resource that can support students in their revision, and such collaboration can be empowering for students.

Class wiki

Start a collaborative class document (e.g. using Google Docs; a document in a shared folder, etc.) and pool knowledge of a particular topic. Make it a condition of the homework that every member of the class has to contribute. The project can be extended to last the length of the topic and students can even be asked to correct funny erroneous details that you have added.

Plan a mark scheme

Students write a mark scheme for an exam question that you have provided. They must ensure the mark scheme is understandable and clearly identifies what is expected of a high quality answer.

Prep

Provide the students with a question that they will answer as the starter task of a subsequent lesson. Their homework is to prepare for that question and ensure that they have plenty of place-specific information ready to go.

Keyword review

Students use their RAG-ing activities to create a list of keywords they need to revise. Each word can be reviewed by writing it in the middle of a page, then surrounding it with notes to help remember it. Can they define the word? Draw the word? Use it in a sentence? List words with similar meanings? List words with opposite meanings?

Sources and weblinks

This page can be downloaded from the online resources, where it includes hyperlinks to the websites listed.

Class of Poets/Silas Zephania: see @SilasZephania (Twitter)

Department for Education (DfE) (2014) *Geography GCSE Subject Content*. London: DfE.

Gapminder: www.gapminder.org

Geographical Association: www.geography.org.uk

GeoGuessr: https://geoguessr.com

Google Docs: https://www.google.com/docs/about

Google Earth: https://earth.google.com/web

Google Expeditions: https://edu.google.com/products/vr-ar/expeditions/?modal_active=none

Hirsch, E. (2016) *Why Knowledge Matters*. Cambridge, MA: Harvard Education Press.

Lemov, D. (2010) *Teach Like A Champion*. San Francisco, CA: Jossey-Bass.

Nuthall, G. (2007) *The Hidden Lives of Learners*. Wellington, NZ: NZCER Press.

Paivio, A. (1971) *Imagery and Verbal Processes*. New York, NY: Holt, Reinhart and Winston.

Smith, J. (2017) *The Lazy Teacher's Handbook* (new edition). Carmarthen: Independent Thinking Press.

The Geological Society: www.geolsoc.org.uk

All websites last accessed 7/1/2019 unless otherwise stated.

Image credits

Book

Page 5: Shaun Flannery; **page 14**: Ted and Jen, Ordnance Survey © Crown Copyright and database rights 2019 Ordnance Survey (100025252) Reproduced with permission of the OS; **page 15**: Freddie Phillips; **page 16**: Shaun Flannery, John Lyon; **page 18**: Bryan Ledgard; **page 19**: F. Delventhal (CC BY 2.0); **page 20**: NASA Goddard MODIS Rapid Response Team, licence free image; **page 21**: Bryan Ledgard; **page 22**: licence free image; **page 23**: Wall Boat (Public Domain); **page 24**: licence free image; **pages 25-28**: Bryan Ledgard; **page 29**: Bryan Ledgard; **page 30**: LukaKikina/Shutterstock, loveordie (CC BY 2.0); **page 31**: Suzanne Baldwin; **pages 32 and 34**: Bryan Ledgard; **page 35**: Shaun Flannery.

PowerPoints

PowerPoint 1: OS map © Crown Copyright and database rights 2019 Ordnance Survey (100025252) Reproduced with permission of the OS; **PowerPoint 3**: slide 11 - F. Delventhal (CC BY 2.0), Keith Kissel (CC BY 2.0), Iain A Robertson (CC BY-SA 2.0); slide 12 - Mike Faherty (CC BY 2.0), Richard Allaway (CC BY 2.0), Bureau of Land Management (CC BY 2.0); **PowerPoint 4**: slide 2 - NASA Goddard MODIS Rapid Response Team; slide 8 - Bryan Ledgard, licence free image, Michael Johnson (CC BY-SA 2.0); **PowerPoint 5**: slide 2 - Jo (CC BY 2.0), pml2008 (CC BY-SA 2.0), Wall Boat (Public Domain), Bryan Ledgard; **PowerPoint 6**: slide 2 - licence free image; slide 5 - Isaac Wedin (CC BY 2.0), Bryan Ledgard, U.S. Department of Agriculture (CC BY 2.0); slide 6 - Bryan Ledgard, Kari Sullivan (CC BY 2.0), Ruth Hartnup (CC BY 2.0); slide 12 - Bryan Ledgard, Marufish (CC BY-SA 2.0); **PowerPoint 7**: slides 2 and 3 - Catherine Owen; **PowerPoint 8**: slides 2 and 3 - David Berkowitz (CC BY 2.0), Xavier Boulenger/Shutterstock, Bryan Ledgard; slides 7 and 8 - licence free images, British Province of Carmelites (CC BY 2.0); **PowerPoint 9**: slide 17 - Catherine Owen.